THE WILD WEST
FAMOUS LAWMEN

by Bonnie Hinman

Content Consultant
Richard Etulain
Professor Emeritus, Department of History
University of New Mexico

Core Library

An Imprint of Abdo Publishing
abdopublishing.com

abdopublishing.com

Published by Abdo Publishing, a division of ABDO, PO Box 398166, Minneapolis, Minnesota 55439. Copyright © 2017 by Abdo Consulting Group, Inc. International copyrights reserved in all countries. No part of this book may be reproduced in any form without written permission from the publisher. Core Library™ is a trademark and logo of Abdo Publishing.

Printed in the United States of America, North Mankato, Minnesota
042016
092016

Cover Photo: The Print Collector/Print Collector/Getty Images
Interior Photos: The Print Collector/Print Collector/Getty Images, 1; Everett Collection, 4; Red Line Editorial, 8, 25; Everett Historical/Shutterstock Images, 9, 12, 18, 23, 45; The Print Collector Heritage Images/Newscom, 16; AP Images, 20; Private Collection/© Look and Learn/Bridgeman Images, 24; John Van Hasselt/Sygma/Corbis, 27; Corbis, 28; Everett Collection/Newscom, 34; American Photographer/Private Collection/Peter Newark American Pictures/Bridgeman Images, 38, 40

Editor: Marie Pearson
Series Designer: Ryan Gale

Cataloging-in-Publication Data
Names: Hinman, Bonnie, author.
Title: Famous lawmen / by Bonnie Hinman.
Description: Minneapolis, MN : Abdo Publishing, [2017] | Series: The wild West
    | Includes bibliographical references and index.
Identifiers: LCCN 2015960504 | ISBN 9781680782554 (lib. bdg.) |
    ISBN 9781680776669 (ebook)
Subjects: LCSH: Peace officers--West (U.S.)--Juvenile literature. | Sheriffs--West
    (U.S.)--Juvenile literature. | Marshals--West (U.S.)--Juvenile literature. |
    Frontier and pioneer life ((U.S.)--Juvenile literature. | Outlaws --West (U.S.)--
    Juvenile literature.
Classification: DDC 978--dc23
LC record available at http://lccn.loc.gov/2015960504

CONTENTS

CHAPTER ONE

THE WILD WEST

In the 1800s, there was a western frontier in the United States. Few Americans lived there. At first the frontier was western Pennsylvania. Then Americans moved farther west. By the time the American Civil War (1861–1865) ended, the West was any place between the Mississippi River and the Pacific Ocean.

Movies about the West often feature shootouts.

Movies depicting the West in the late 1800s often show a lawless land where shootouts, cattle rustling, and murders happened every day. Movies and television shows called it the Wild West. But the truth about the West is a bit different.

Arrest records from that time show that some of the most common crimes were assault, drunkenness, gambling, burglary, and carrying concealed weapons. Murder was much lower on the list of crimes.

The Lawmen

Even though lawmen did not have to catch murderers every day, they still had plenty of work. There were usually three

Justice in the Old West

Lawmen captured many criminals, but judges and juries did not always deal out justice fairly. Some judges and juries could be bribed to come to a certain verdict. And punishment was often minimal for crimes such as assault. A man might only pay a fine or serve a few days in jail. Self-defense was a common excuse for a shooting. Many were found not guilty because they claimed they had killed a man in self-defense.

different kinds of lawmen in the West: regional US marshals, county sheriffs, and city marshals. All had assistants, who were usually called deputies. City marshals were also called constables or police chiefs.

Regional US marshals enforced national laws. These included laws about army desertion and theft of government property. A county sheriff was appointed or elected by county officials. His jurisdiction was the entire county. He enforced county laws. Towns employed city marshals. City marshals were appointed or elected by a city council. City marshals enforced state and local laws in one town or city. Unlike a sheriff, a city marshal's jurisdiction ended at the city limits. A city marshal might ask for

PERSPECTIVES
No Catch, No Pay

A US marshal's life was not easy. He was often not paid if he did not catch an outlaw or if he killed the outlaw. It did not matter how far the lawman had traveled or how long he had searched. If he wanted to be paid, he needed to be successful.

Position	Laws Enforced	Jurisdiction
US Marshal	federal laws	region
County Sheriff	county laws	county
City Marshal Constable Police Chief	state and local laws	city

Lawmen of the West
Examine the chart. Which position enforces laws in the smallest area? Which do you think had the most power?

the sheriff's help when he felt he could not handle a problem by himself.

Scandal and Skill

Old Western movies got something else wrong about the West. Many movies showed lawmen as honest citizens. There were some lawmen like that. But others had shaky reputations, such as those who were reformed outlaws or gunfighters. And some were more reformed than others.

If a man was known for being good with a revolver, town officials often thought that was qualification enough to be a lawman. Some criminals

Sometimes being good with a gun was enough for someone to become a lawman.

would avoid a town if the sheriff or marshal could handle a gun. Often officials did not care if a lawman had been arrested before he was hired to uphold the law. And some lawmen continued to commit crimes while on the job.

The more famous of the lawmen moved from town to town. If one failed to be reelected or was fired, he packed up and moved to another town. With a reputation as a tough man and a good shot, he was likely to get another job as a lawman.

The West was not always full of gunfights and crime. Almost every town in the West had laws against carrying guns in town. Lawmen kept order in their towns or counties. Land, gold, or a new start drew Americans west. A peaceful town was the best way to attract these dreamers who settled the Wild West.

According to the editor of the Coolidge, Kansas, newspaper, city marshals needed specific qualifications. In the July 17, 1886, edition of *Border Ruffian*, the editor defined a city marshal as:

> *having the skin of a rhinocerous, a bullet-proof head, who can see all around him, run faster than a horse, and is not afraid of anything in hades . . . a man who can shoot like [Captain A.] Bogardus, and would rather kill four or five whisky-drinking, gambling hoodlums before breakfast than to eat without exercise. Such a man can get a job in this town at reasonable wages, and if he put off climbing the gold stair for a few years may get his name in a ten-cent novel.*

Source: The West: From Lewis and Clark to Wounded Knee, The Turbulent Story of the Settling of Frontier America. *Ed. William C. Davis and Joseph G. Rosa. New York: Smithmark, 1994. Print. 116.*

Back it Up

This author is making a point about city marshals. He used evidence to support his point. Write a paragraph describing the point the author is making. Then write down two or three pieces of evidence the author used to make his point.

CHAPTER TWO

WILD BILL HICKOK AND PAT GARRETT

James Butler Hickok was born on May 27, 1837. His skill with guns began when he was a young boy. In his early teenage years, he traded some possessions for a gun. He practiced shooting in all his spare time.

During the American Civil War, Hickok served in the Union Army. He became famous as a scout and a

Hickok became a lawman after the American Civil War.

spy. He may have first been called "Wild Bill" because of his adventures in the Civil War.

Hickok's reputation as a fast gun grew after the war. Newspaper articles called him "The Prince of the Pistoleers." His skill with a handgun was legendary. Sometimes journalists exaggerated Hickok's shooting abilities. Reporters said he could hit a dime edge-on. Many years later, experts tested this claim and declared it impossible. But it was true that he could fire two guns at the same time. He seldom missed his target.

Hickok held several jobs as a lawman. In 1866 he became a deputy US marshal in Kansas. In 1869 he was elected sheriff of Ellis County in Kansas.

Wild West Shows

Wild Bill Hickok was friends with Buffalo Bill Cody. Cody's famous Wild West show was the most well known of its kind. It was a huge spectacle of cowboys, sharpshooters, and animals such as buffalo and elk. The show was partially based on fact. But much of it was inaccurate. Some performers, such as Annie Oakley, were not from the West. Buffalo Bill's show ran from 1883 to 1916.

Then he became city marshal of Abilene, Kansas, in 1871.

During his life, Hickok killed five to ten men. This was far fewer than newspapers and magazines at the time claimed. Hickok said he had only killed in self-defense or as an official duty.

Hickok liked to drink and gamble. His bad habits led to his downfall. On August 2, 1876, he was playing poker with other gamblers in the Number Ten saloon in Deadwood, Dakota Territory. An unhappy fellow gambler shot Hickok, killing him.

Pat Garrett

Patrick Floyd Garrett was born on June 5, 1850, in Alabama. He grew up in Louisiana. He left home at 19 to become a cowboy and hunt buffalo in Texas.

Garrett became a lawman in November 1880. He was elected sheriff of Lincoln County, New Mexico. His first job as sheriff was to track down famous outlaw Billy the Kid. Billy worked as a gunman and had killed a couple of men. Even before Garrett

Garrett, *left*, became sheriff of Lincoln County in 1880.

officially took office, he rode out with a posse of men to find Billy. The chase ended in a gun battle. Garrett and his posse captured Billy and some of his gang in December 1880. Billy was sent to Mesilla, New Mexico, to stand trial for murder.

Billy was found guilty in April 1881 and sentenced to die by hanging. The hanging was scheduled for

May 13, 1881. But Billy escaped. He killed two guards on April 28. It took Garrett three months to find Billy again. This time he took no chances. He shot and killed Billy in Fort Sumner, New Mexico, on July 14, 1881.

Garrett went on to become a Texas Ranger. Texas Rangers were state law enforcement officers. Then he became a sheriff for Doña Ana County in New Mexico. But killing Billy the Kid overshadowed everything else Garrett did as a lawman.

PERSPECTIVES
Billy the Kid as a Folk Hero

Billy the Kid is one of the most famous outlaws in history. Orphaned at 15, Billy and a friend burglarized a Chinese laundry. Eventually Billy began stealing horses and learned to use a six-shooter. Newspapers reported he killed more than 20 men. Only four have been confirmed. In spite of his reputation as a killer, many people saw him as a hero of sorts. Some have even compared him to Robin Hood. Billy worked on a ranch in 1878. Two men killed the ranch owner. Billy and several others killed both men in revenge.

Garrett, *right*, killed Billy the Kid after Billy escaped jail. Newspapers at the time likely exaggerated the number of people Billy had killed.

Sheriff
PAT GARRETT

"BILLY *the* KID" with a record of 21 victims was only 21 years old when he was killed at Ft. Sumner by Sheriff Pat Garrett in 1881.

Garrett's disagreeable personality made him likely to find trouble everywhere he went. Wayne Brazel leased land on Garrett's ranch. Brazel grazed goats there. But Garrett did not like goats. He wanted to remove the goats. He found a man who would lease land to graze cattle instead. On February 29, 1908, Garrett was on his way to arrange the deal when he was shot and killed. Brazel confessed to killing Garrett. He said it was in self-defense. The court found him not guilty of Garrett's murder.

FURTHER EVIDENCE

This chapter includes information about Wild Bill Hickok and Pat Garrett. Review the chapter and find the main points made about both lawmen. Look at the following websites and see if you can find quotes about the two men. Does what you found support the main point of the chapter or add new details?

Hickok and Garrett

mycorelibrary.com/lawmen

CHAPTER THREE

WYATT EARP AND DOC HOLLIDAY

Wyatt Earp is perhaps the most famous US lawman. He had four brothers. They often stuck together. Virgil and Morgan were both well-known lawmen themselves.

Earp became constable, or city marshal, in Lamar, Missouri, in 1870. The town's biggest problems were pigs running loose in the streets and drunks. Earp

Earp is still famous today for his work as a lawman.

worked one case of arson in Lamar. He left Lamar shortly after his young wife, Urilla, died suddenly.

In the years that followed, Earp hunted buffalo and became a deputy city marshal in Dodge City, Kansas. He dealt cards in saloons. After moving to Tombstone, Arizona, he became a deputy sheriff. His brother Virgil became Tombstone's city marshal in 1881. Tombstone was where Earp would make his legacy.

Tuberculosis

Another name once used for tuberculosis was consumption. This was because the disease caused extreme weight loss in its victims. It seemed to consume them. It had been a common illness since ancient times. Some researchers say that by the beginning of the 1800s, tuberculosis had killed one of every seven people who had ever lived. Tuberculosis is caused by bacteria. There was no effective drug treatment for the disease until antibiotics were discovered in the 1940s.

Doc Holliday

John Henry Holliday's parents were wealthy. He went to dental school. He earned the nickname Doc upon graduation. Holliday practiced dentistry in several towns, but he

Holliday was good friends with Earp and followed Earp to Tombstone.

suffered from tuberculosis. He was often ill, and he had trouble keeping patients. He started gambling and drinking instead. He was known for his quick temper when gambling.

Holliday and Earp became friends in Dodge City, Kansas, in 1877. Holliday moved to Tombstone, Arizona, in September 1880, several months after Earp arrived there. Holliday's time as a lawman was

The Earp brothers and Holliday confronted Cowboy gang members on Fremont Street.

served entirely as a deputy to one or another of the Earp brothers. Holliday got into trouble regularly, mostly from gambling, drinking liquor, and fighting.

Gunfight at the O.K. Corral

Earp and Holliday are known for a famous gunfight in Tombstone. A gang of outlaws called the Cowboys had robbed a stagecoach near Tombstone in March 1881. Then on October 26, 1881, some members of the Cowboy gang came to Tombstone to drink and gamble. Cowboy Ike Clanton made several threats against the Earp brothers. That afternoon Wyatt, Virgil, Morgan, and Holliday, who was a deputy at the time, marched down the street toward the O.K.

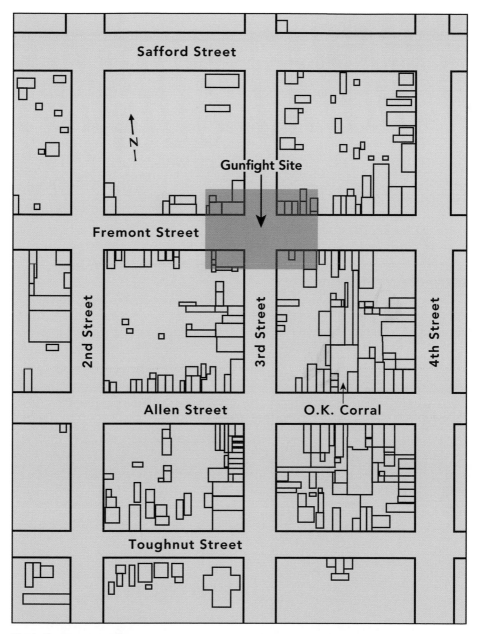

Tombstone Map

This map shows where the Gunfight at the O.K. Corral took place in Tombstone, Arizona, October 26, 1881. Find the O.K. Corral on the map. Where is the O.K. Corral in relation to the gunfight?

Corral. At the same time, Cowboy gang members made their way to Fremont Street. They met near a boarding house rather than at the O.K. Corral. One of the lawmen fired. Then everyone was shooting. The famous and misnamed Gunfight at the O.K. Corral was over in less than a minute.

Outlaws Tom and Frank McLaury and Billy Clanton were killed. Ike Clanton, who had started the trouble, escaped. Holliday was grazed by a bullet, and Wyatt Earp was uninjured.

After the Showdown

In March 1882, Morgan Earp was killed. Holliday rode with Wyatt Earp to find the killers. A district

PERSPECTIVES
A Justified Fight?

After the O.K. Corral gunfight, the Tombstone sheriff attempted to arrest Earp. But citizens defended Earp's actions. So the sheriff did not arrest him right away. Still, some townspeople did not agree. They thought the Earps should have waited longer before firing. Ike Clanton finally filed a murder charge against the Earps and Holliday. The judge found them not guilty.

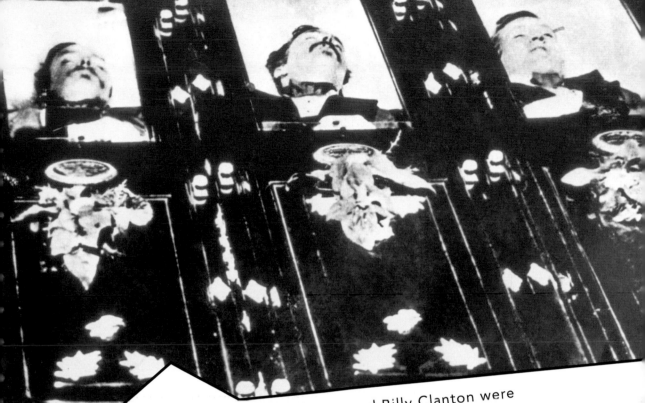

Tom McLaury, Frank McLaury, and Billy Clanton were killed in the Gunfight at the O.K. Corral.

judge gave Earp and his posse warrants for the arrest of the men. But Earp killed three of the suspects and became wanted for murder. He escaped to Colorado with Holliday. There Holliday's tuberculosis worsened. He died in Glenwood Springs, Colorado, on November 8, 1887.

Earp got married that same year. He traveled, participated in horse racing, and ran saloons. He died in January 1929. He was 80 years old.

CHAPTER FOUR

BAT MASTERSON AND HIS BROTHERS

Bartholomew Masterson was born November 26, 1853, in Canada. He later went by Bat Masterson. Masterson and his brothers Ed and Jim became buffalo hunters. During their buffalo-hunting days, the Masterson brothers met Wyatt Earp. Earp maintained a friendship with Masterson throughout their lifetimes. Earp suggested that Masterson and his brother Jim become law officers.

Masterson, right, and Earp, left, were friends throughout their lives.

Buffalo Hunting

Buffalo are actually correctly referred to as bison. Early settlers called them buffalo because they looked like the buffalo found in India and Africa. After the Civil War, "buffalo" hunting became a common way to make a living. Plains Native Americans relied on bison for food, shelter, and clothing. Americans moved West after the Civil War. Many thought that getting rid of the bison would also get rid of the Native Americans. This would open up land for white settlers. Thousands of bison were killed each year. The bison were mostly gone from the plains by 1884. With so few bison, the Plains Native Americans were weakened. They were less able to fight the US government in order to keep their land.

Lawman and Sports Reporter

The Masterson brothers, including Ed, took Earp's advice. Ed worked his way up to city marshal of Dodge City, Kansas, in 1877. Bat Masterson worked as undersheriff for Ford County, Kansas, until he was elected sheriff in October 1877. Dodge City was home to the Ford County government. Masterson spent much of his time there. He was not in charge of the law in Dodge City. But he helped his brother when needed. Masterson's younger brother Jim served as his deputy.

In April 1878, Ed was shot in the Lady Gay Saloon in Dodge City. Masterson rushed to the saloon and stayed with his brother until Ed died about 30 minutes later.

Masterson became a deputy US Marshal in 1879. He was appointed city marshal of Trinidad, Colorado, in April 1882. While there, Doc Holliday was arrested in Colorado for a murder he allegedly committed in Arizona. The authorities in Arizona hated him. He had helped Earp kill Morgan's suspected murderers. If Holliday was sent to Arizona, he would be killed. It would not matter whether he was guilty of the murder.

Earp asked Masterson to help free Holliday. Masterson did not particularly like Holliday, but he persuaded Colorado's governor to block Holliday's return to Arizona. Holliday was released on bond and never put on trial.

In his later years, Masterson spent much of his time gambling and promoting sporting events. He worked with horse races and prize fights. He married singer and dancer Emma Walters on November 21, 1891. In 1902 the couple moved to New York City. Masterson became a sports reporter for the *Morning Telegraph*. He died at his desk there on October 25, 1921.

When Bat Masterson died, tributes poured into the office of the *Morning Telegraph* newspaper. Masterson's friend William Jerome praised Masterson with poetry. The following is a stanza from a poem Jerome wrote in honor of Masterson:

Good-bye, Bat,
They never heard you blat
About the things you did out West—
You wasn't built like that.
That great big golden heart of yours,
It wouldn't harm a cat.
Sweet as a "gal," so long, old pal.
Good-bye, Bat.

Source: Robert K. DeArment. Bat Masterson: The Man and the Legend. *1ˢᵗ ed.*
Norman, OK: University of Oklahoma Press, 1979. Print. 398–399.

Consider Your Audience

This poem was written for Masterson's friends and uses phrases we probably would not use today. In a paragraph or two or in a poem, write a tribute to Masterson that praises the same qualities as the poem's author did. Write the tribute in words that your parents or your teacher might use today.

CHAPTER FIVE

THE THREE GUARDSMEN

The Three Guardsmen were legendary lawmen in the 1890s. Chris Madsen, Bill Tilghman, and Heck Thomas made up the trio. Newspapers and magazines of the time gave them their name. The three helped "guard," or protect, citizens in Indian Territory. The Territory, which was part of present-day Oklahoma, could be a lawless place. The Guardsmen helped restore order. According to many writers and

Tilghman was one of three lawmen referred to as the Three Guardsmen.

the Guardsmen themselves, the three arrested more than 300 outlaws during their careers.

But some historians believe the Guardsmen's story is quite different. The legends said that the three men killed or captured many outlaws, such as members of the Dalton Gang and the Doolin Gang. Records tell a different story. The Three Guardsmen did pursue the gangs at different times. But only Thomas killed one Doolin Gang member. Madsen and Tilghman made a movie called *The Passing of the Oklahoma Outlaws* in 1915. The film may have started the legends.

The real Three Guardsmen seemed to love the spotlight. They were lawmen during a dangerous time in the West. They wanted to sound even braver.

Tilghman, Madsen, and Thomas

Bill Tilghman first worked as a buffalo hunter in Kansas and Colorado. He became a deputy sheriff in 1874. He held jobs as deputy city marshal and city marshal.

Tilghman broke the law almost as often as he made others keep it. But he was not always convicted. He was arrested for horse theft and train robbery in Kansas. The charges were later dropped. Despite his history with the law, he became a deputy US marshal in 1892. He held that position for several years.

Chris Madsen was born in Denmark on February 25, 1851. He immigrated to the United States in 1876. He joined the US Army soon after

The US Marshals Service

George Washington appointed the first US marshals on September 24, 1789, and there are 94 US marshals in service today. They were the first federal law enforcement officers. The deputy or assistant marshals have always served warrants, made arrests, and handled prisoners. In the West, they were often the only lawmen available when a new town did not have a sheriff or other official. US marshals also assisted local authorities when called upon. It was and still is a dangerous job. The first US marshal was killed in 1794. More than 200 US marshals, deputy marshals, special duty marshals, and marshal guards have since lost their lives in the line of duty.

Madsen often embellished stories about his life.

his arrival. While in the army, he spent five months in Wyoming Territorial Prison for theft.

Madsen became a deputy US marshal in 1891. He served in Oklahoma Territory, the Western District of Missouri, Indian Territory, and finally in the state of Oklahoma. He earned a reputation as a tough, quick shot. He spent time hunting the Dalton outlaw gang. The Daltons were famous train robbers. In

1892 the gang decided to rob two banks at one time in Coffeyville, Kansas. The townspeople killed all members of the Dalton Gang except Emmett Dalton. Madsen was not present at that fight. Dalton served 14 years in prison.

Madsen often exaggerated stories of his life. He claimed he was in the French Foreign Legion before coming to America. The claim was false. But Madsen told reporters what they wanted to hear. Newspapers and magazines at that time were not as interested in the facts as they were in telling an exciting story.

Henry Andrew "Heck" Thomas was a dedicated lawman. He became a policeman in Atlanta,

PERSPECTIVES
The Dalton Gang

After Emmett Dalton's release from prison, he became a celebrity and acted in several Western movies. He advised Western moviemakers about historical details for their films. Dalton claimed that his older brother Bob had been cheated out of money owed him. That had sparked their life of crime. But after his time in prison, Dalton spoke against a life of crime.

Thomas was known as a fearless lawman.

Georgia, after the Civil War. In 1886 he became a deputy US marshal in Fort Smith, Arkansas. He served as a deputy marshal for courts in Oklahoma Territory and Fort Smith, Indian Territory, until 1901. He brought in as many as a dozen prisoners at a time. From 1885 to 1901, he worked off and on with Madsen and Tilghman. While Thomas went along with the embellished stories, he did not add to them.

The Guardsmen's Legacy

Tilghman is most famous for capturing Bill Doolin, leader of the Doolin Gang of outlaws. All three of the Guardsmen chased the Doolin Gang. Tilghman captured Doolin in January 1896. Doolin later escaped before the trial. Thomas caught and killed him over a month later.

The Three Guardsmen's successes may in part be legend. But they were part of an important generation of lawmen. These lawmen were vital to the westward movement of settlers in the late 1800s.

EXPLORE ONLINE

This chapter contains some information about the crimes and false tales of the Three Guardsmen. The website below gives more information on the three men. Contrast the information in this article with the information given in the chapter. In what way does the website article give a different view of the Guardsmen than the book?

The Three Guardsmen

mycorelibrary.com/lawmen

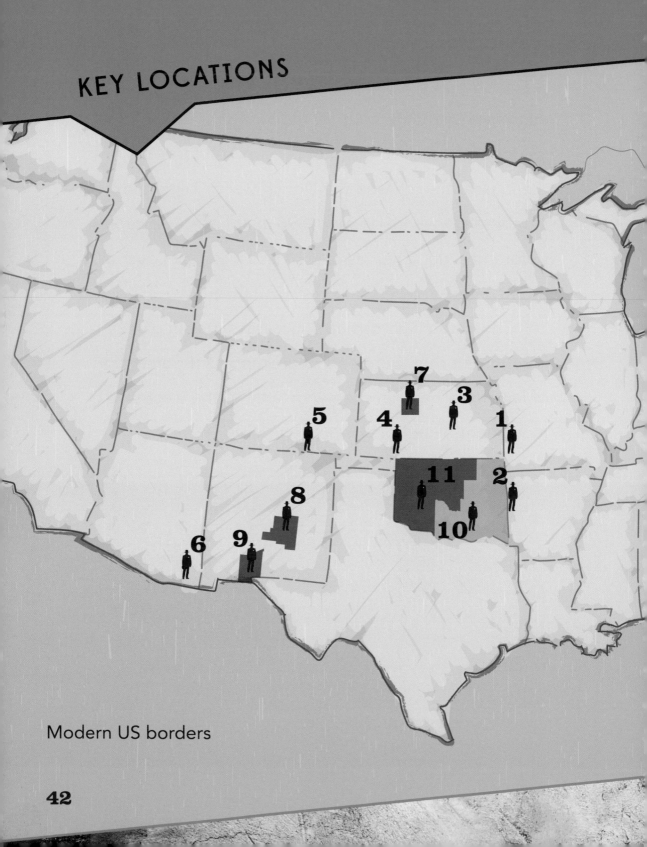

Modern US borders

Cities and Counties Lawmen Protected

1. Lamar, Missouri

2. Fort Smith, Arkansas

3. Abilene, Kansas

4. Dodge City, Kansas

5. Trinidad, Colorado

6. Tombstone, Arizona

7. Ellis County, Kansas

8. Lincoln County, New Mexico

9. Doña Ana County, New Mexico

10. Indian Territory 1891

11. Oklahoma Territory 1891

STOP AND THINK

You Are There

In Chapter Three, the Earp brothers and Doc Holliday took part in the famous gun battle at the O.K. Corral. Pretend you were watching the gunfight. Write a letter to a friend describing it. Use details of sight, sound, and smell to help your friend understand what it was like to watch the famous gun battle.

Take a Stand

In this book we discover that not all lawmen always followed the law. They sometimes committed crimes themselves. Do you think this happens today? Would it be harder for a person to commit crimes as a lawman or -woman today? Would the constant news coverage today make a difference? Why or why not?

Dig Deeper

Several of the lawmen in this book were buffalo
hunters as young men. With an adult's help, find
a source that tells about a buffalo hunt. Write a
description of the different jobs that had to be done
before a buffalo hide could be sent to a buyer.

Tell the Tale

If you were going to make a movie about the Old
West, what story would you want to tell? Write several
paragraphs telling what characters you would include
and what they would do in the movie.

GLOSSARY

cattle rustling
stealing cattle

frontier
a distant part of a country where few people live

gunfighter
an outlaw or lawman who was highly skilled with a gun and used it to solve arguments

jurisdiction
the extent or range of authority or control over an area

marshal
a US marshal is a federal law officer, but a town marshal is only responsible for enforcing the law inside a particular town

posse
a group of people a sheriff assembles to keep the peace

saloon
a restaurant and bar

sheriff
the highest law enforcement official of a county

stagecoach
a large carriage pulled by horses that carried passengers and mail along established routes

warrants
documents that authorize a lawman to arrest someone

LEARN MORE

Books

Fleischman, Sid. *The Trouble Begins at 8: A Life of Mark Twain in the Wild, Wild West*. New York: Greenwillow Books, 2008.

Harrison, David. *Cowboys: Voices in the Western Wind*. Honesdale, PA: Wordsong, 2012.

Yasuda, Anita. *Notorious Outlaws*. Minneapolis, MN: Abdo Publishing, 2016.

Websites

To learn more about the Wild West, visit **booklinks.abdopublishing.com**. These links are routinely monitored and updated to provide the most current information available.

Visit **mycorelibrary.com** for free additional tools for teachers and students.

INDEX

ABOUT THE AUTHOR

Bonnie Hinman has written more than 40 books, most of them nonfiction. Two of her latest books were about the War of 1812 and World War I. Hinman lives in Southwest Missouri with her husband Bill, near her children and five grandchildren.